Meet Our New Student From

TANZANIA

Ann Weil

Mitchell Lane
PUBLISHERS

P.O. Box 196
Hockessin, Delaware 19707
Visit us on the web: www.mitchelllane.com
Comments? email us: mitchelllane@mitchelllane.com

Meet Our New Student From

Australia • China • Colombia • Great Britain • Haiti • Israel • Korea • Malaysia • Mexico • New Zealand • Nigeria • **Tanzania**

For Sarah Messenger, Paul Weber, and most of all Leyeyo

Copyright © 2009 by Mitchell Lane Publishers

PUBLISHER'S NOTE: The facts on which the story in this book is based have been thoroughly researched. Documentation of such research can be found on page 44. While every possible effort has been made to ensure accuracy, the publisher will not assume liability for damages caused by inaccuracies in the data, and makes no warranty on the accuracy of the information contained herein.

To reflect current usage, we have chosen to use the secular era designations BCE ("before the common era") and CE ("of the common era") instead of the traditional designations BC ("before Christ") and AD (*anno Domini*, "in the year of the Lord").

Printing 1 2 3 4 5 6 7 8 9

Library of Congress Cataloging-in-Publication Data

Weil, Ann.
    Meet our new student from Tanzania / by Ann Weil.
       p. cm. — (A Robbie reader)
    Includes bibliographical references and index.
    ISBN 978-1-58415-656-7 (library bound)
    1. Tanzania—Juvenile literature. I. Title.
DT438.W45 2008
967.8—dc22

2008002819

PLB

CONTENTS

Dar es Salaam ("Place of Peace") is the largest city in Tanzania. About 2.5 million people live there. It sits on a big natural harbor of the Indian Ocean. Dar es Salaam was the capital of Tanzania until 1974. Although the capital was moved to the much smaller city of Dodoma in the center of the country, Dar es Salaam is still the country's most important city for trade, transportation, services, and manufacturing.

A New
Soccer Player

Chapter **1**

Jack ran to the end of his driveway, hoping he wasn't too late. His backpack bounced as he pumped his arms. Just as he reached his mailbox, the school bus pulled up.

"Late again, Jack?" asked the bus driver with a smile.

"Good morning," said Jack, panting. What a relief! He sat down next to his friend Luke. They were in the same third-grade class at Putney Elementary School.

It was the second week of school and the leaves were just beginning to change. Next month, people from all over would be driving through his little Vermont village to enjoy the fall colors. Leaf peepers, they were called. Every year around that time, Jack and Luke had a contest to see who could spot more out-of-state license plates. But today they had other things to think about. There was a soccer game that afternoon. It was their first of the season.

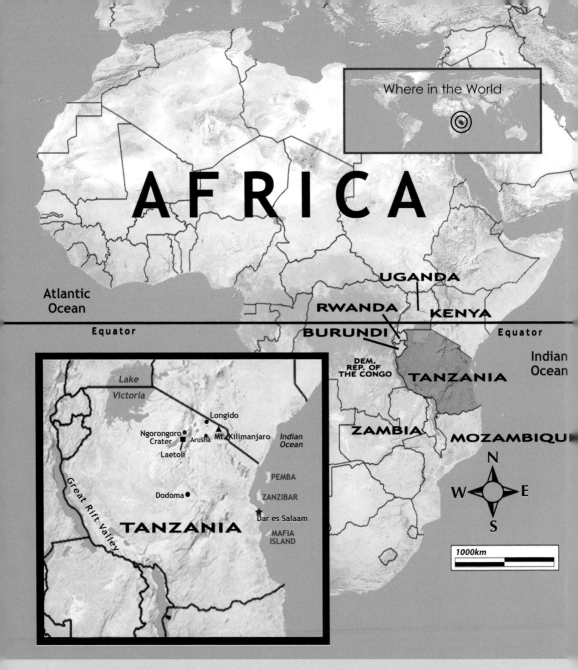

Where in the World

AFRICA

Atlantic
Ocean

UGANDA

RWANDA

KENYA

Equator

BURUNDI

Equator

DEM.
REP. OF
THE CONGO

TANZANIA

Indian
Ocean

ZAMBIA

MOZAMBIQUE

Lake
Victoria

Longido

Ngorongoro
Crater
Arusha
Mt. Kilimanjaro
Indian
Ocean

Laetoli

PEMBA

Dodoma

ZANZIBAR

Great Rift Valley

TANZANIA

Dar es Salaam

MAFIA
ISLAND

N

W   E

S

1000km

FACTS ABOUT THE UNITED REPUBLIC OF TANZANIA

Total Area
364,900 square miles
(includes 22,805 square miles of water)

Population
39,384,223 (July 2007 estimate)

Capital City
Dodoma

Monetary Unit
Tanzanian shilling

Religions
Mainland: Christianity, Islam, indigenous
beliefs
Zanzibar: more than 99 percent Muslim
(Islam)

Languages
Kiswahili or Swahili; English (for commerce);
and some Arabic

Chief Exports
Gold, coffee, cashew nuts, manufactures,
cotton

"We beat them last year," said Jack. He remembered the game well. He had scored the winning goal.

"But I heard they've got three new players," said Luke.

"I wish we had more soccer players at our school," added Jack.

The bus stopped in front of the school building, and everyone got off. Jack and Luke tossed their jackets into their cubbies and made it to homeroom just as the bell rang.

Ms. Griffith was writing something on the board. "Good morning, class," she said. "I have an important announcement to make."

Jack thought the teacher was going to talk about the soccer game that afternoon. That was the only thing on his mind.

"We are getting a new student next week," Ms. Griffith continued. "He is from Tanzania, and his name is . . ." She wrote *Saitoti Eliapenda* on the board. "Sy-ah-toh-tee El-ee-ah-pen-dah," she said slowly.

"That's a cool name," said Katie.

"It sure is a long name," added Lisa. She repeated the nine syllables softly.

"After we learn how to say his name," Ms. Griffith went on, "we will learn about his country, Tanzania, which is in East Africa. We will also learn about his people, the Maasai." She wrote *Maasai* on the board. The class repeated the word: "Mah-SY."

"Are the Maasai the only people in Tanzania?" asked Luke.

"The Maasai are just one group of **tribal** people who live in Tanzania," explained Ms. Griffith. "There are other tribal people with different customs than the Maasai. These different groups tend to live separately."

"Does everyone live in villages?" asked Anja.

"Not everyone, but more African people live in villages than in cities. Dar es Salaam is the largest city in Tanzania." She wrote that name on the board. "It was the capital, and has more people and more jobs than any other city in Tanzania. Another city is Dodoma. Dodoma is the new capital of Tanzania." She walked over to the wall map. "Dodoma is in the center of the country. Another city in Tanzania is Arusha. Arusha is here, near the border with Kenya, which is another country in Africa. It's a big tourist center. Arusha is a base for people who are going on **safaris**. What animals would you see on an African safari?" she asked the class.

"Lions!"

"Elephants!"

Ms. Griffith wrote the names of the animals on the board.

"Hippos."

"Rhinoceroses."

The list grew longer.

Jack raised his hand. "Yes, Jack?" said Ms. Griffith.

Most Maasai men shave their heads. They wear jewelry and hair extensions as decorations. Red is the Maasai color. Both Maasai men and women wear this color.

The city of Arusha is home to about 300,000 people. It is in the shadow of Mount Meru, an active volcano that last erupted in 1910. Arusha is a busy "safari town," where people from around the world start their adventure to see the exotic animals that roam the African plains.

A safari road cuts through a park in Africa. Most people go on a safari to see the animals. Many take pictures to show friends and family back home. But others on safari might hunt and kill the animals for sport. The animals in parks are protected. It is against the law for people to hunt or kill them there.

"Do they play soccer in Tan-zuh-nee-ah?" He said the name of the country slowly and carefully.

Ms. Griffith smiled. "Yes, Jack, they do. In fact, soccer is their national sport."

"Yes!" Jack and Luke cheered together.

This trail of footprints was discovered in Laetoli, Tanzania, in 1978. Scientists believe that the humans who made these footprints lived more than three and a half million years ago.

Million-Year-Old
Footprints

Chapter

2

Tanzania is a young country with a long history. The name Tanzania only came into use in 1964, but this part of East Africa was populated by humans millions of years ago. This area is known as the "cradle of humanity" because it is likely that the first people on Earth lived there.

Million-Year-Old Footprints

Scientists believe that some of the first people on Earth walked in East Africa. In Tanzania, in a place called Laetoli, there are **fossils** of human footprints. Ash from volcanoes was soft when these early humans walked across it. Later, the ground, with the footprints in it, became hard as rock. These fossils date from more than 3.5 million years ago!

Hunter-Gatherers

The earliest African people were hunter-gatherers. This describes how they found food to eat. They hunted animals for meat. They also gathered plant foods, including roots, seeds, and fruit. They did not live in one place. Instead they moved from place to place, following the food supply.

Arab Culture Comes to East Africa

Traders from Arabia came to East Africa almost a thousand years ago, in the 1100s. They traveled by ship, up and down the coast, and began to settle there. Zanzibar, an island, had calm bays. These were useful ports for Arab trading ships.

The African people picked up some of the Arab language and culture. Out of this mixture came the Swahili (swah-HEE-lee) language, which is the official language of Tanzania. It is spoken by more than 30 million people.

The Arab traders were Muslim. Muslim people follow the religion of Islam. Many native Africans adopted this religion as their own. Today, about one-third of Tanzanians who live on the mainland are Muslim. Most of the people on the island of Zanzibar are Muslim.

Europeans Arrive in East Africa

People in Europe wanted to buy spices from Asia. Kings and queens in Europe wanted to control this important trade. Many ships left Europe in search of an easy sea route to "the Indies."

Vasco da Gama was an explorer from Portugal, which is a country in Europe. During 1497 and 1498, da Gama sailed around Africa to India. He was the first person from Europe known to do this. His historic voyage opened Portuguese trade with India. The coast of East Africa was on the trade route. The Portuguese won control of this area, and ruled it for more than 200 years.

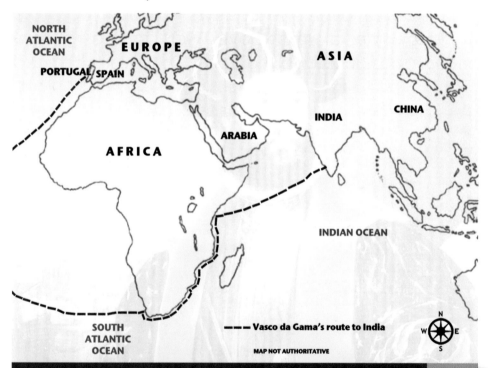

Vasco da Gama sailed around the Cape of Good Hope near the southern tip of Africa. This was a long, dangerous voyage. He stopped in many places on Africa's east coast before continuing to India.

The Sultan of Zanzibar and the Slave Trade

Arab **sultans** ruled the island of Zanzibar in the 1700s and 1800s. They traded with African chiefs on the mainland. The sultans traded guns for slaves and ivory (elephant tusks).

Arab slave traders set up slave stations inland, many miles from the coast. Some African chiefs raided other villages and took the people as slaves. Then they handed them over to Arab slave traders.

The people taken as slaves were forced to carry heavy loads of ivory to the coast. They were chained

The Sultan's Palace at Zanzibar is also known as the "House of Wonders." It was built in 1883 by the third sultan of Zanzibar.

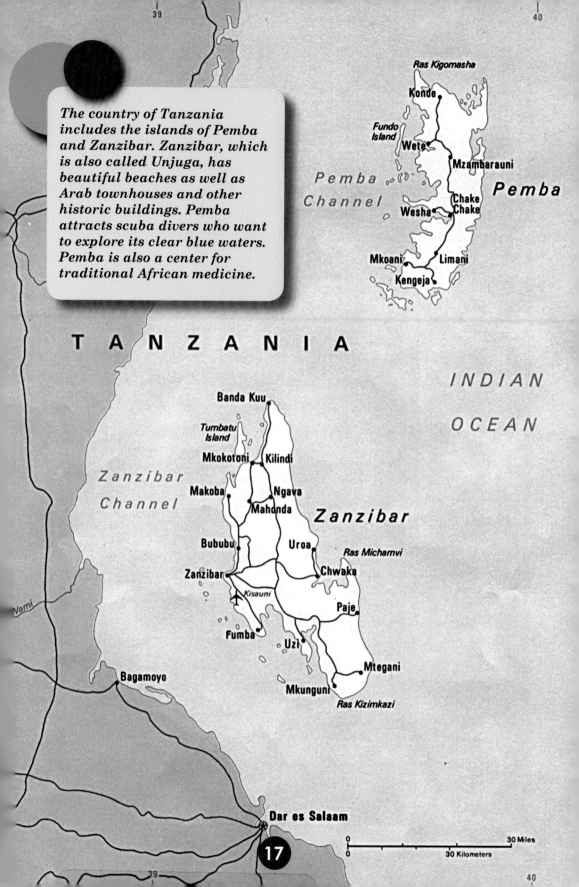

The country of Tanzania includes the islands of Pemba and Zanzibar. Zanzibar, which is also called Unjuga, has beautiful beaches as well as Arab townhouses and other historic buildings. Pemba attracts scuba divers who want to explore its clear blue waters. Pemba is also a center for traditional African medicine.

Ras Kigomasha

Konde

Fundo
Island

Wete

Mzambarauni

*Pemba
Channel*

Pemba

Wesha

Chake
Chake

Mkoani

Limani

Kengeja

T A N Z A N I A

*INDIAN
OCEAN*

Banda Kuu

*Tumbatu
Island*

Mkokotoni

Kilindi

*Zanzibar
Channel*

Makoba

Ngava

Mahonda

Zanzibar

Bububu

Uroa

Zanzibar

Ras Michamvi

Chwaka

Kisauni

Paje

Fumba

Uzi

Mtegani

Bagamoyo

Mkunguni

Ras Kizimkazi

Vami

Dar es Salaam

17

30 Miles

30 Kilometers

together and brutally whipped along the way. If any were too weak to go on, they were left to die alone.

When they reached the coast, the slaves (and the ivory) were put onto ships for the trip to Zanzibar. The slaves were packed so tightly together that some could not breathe and died on the way. Sick slaves were thrown into the sea.

After the ships landed, the surviving slaves were washed, wiped with oil, and dressed. Then they were taken to the slave market in Zanzibar town. Buyers looked them over. They examined their teeth and muscles. Slaves who were bought were loaded onto other ships, many bound for China, India, and Arabia.

The Zanzibar slave trade was huge. By 1750, more than 3,000 slaves were passing through Zanzibar each year. By 1800, about 8,000 people were being sold as slaves each year. The Zanzibar slave market was finally closed in 1873, after slavery was made illegal.

British Rule, Then Independence

After World War I (1914–1918), the British government controlled Zanzibar and the mainland portion of Tanzania, which was then called Tanganyika. Tanganyika became **independent** in 1961. In 1964, Zanzibar joined Tanganyika to form the United Republic of Tanzania. Two smaller islands, Pemba and Mafia, are also part of Tanzania.

Far left: Julius Nyerere, the first Tanzanian president. Standing left to right: Benjamin Mkapa, outgoing president of Tanzania; Jakaya Kikwete, incoming president of Tanzania; and Ali Hassan Mwinyi, former president of Tanzania.

Name	Took Office	Left Office
Julius Nyerere	October 29, 1964	November 5, 1985
Ali Hassan Mwinyi	November 5, 1985	November 23, 1995
Benjamin Mkapa	November 23, 1995	December 21, 2005
Jakaya Kikwete	December 21, 2005	~

The Government of Tanzania

Tanzania is a democracy. People vote to elect their president. For the first twenty years after independence, Tanzania was a **socialist** state. There was only one **political party.** Now, the economy is based more on **capitalism**, like the economy in the United States. There are also more political parties.

Tanzania

Mount Kilimanjaro is on the border of Tanzania and Kenya, just south of the equator. It stands alone, rising steeply to its snowy peaks. This sleeping volcano has not erupted for 100,000 years, but it was probably quite active and dangerous when the first people lived in that part of East Africa.

The Land and Animals
of Tanzania

Chapter

Tanzania is more than twice the size of California. It is on the east coast of Africa, a little south of the **equator**. Places close to the equator have warm weather all year round. Tanzania does not have the four seasons found in North America. The coast is hot and wet. The **plains** are hot and very dry. There is, however, one place to find snow year-round in Tanzania. It's a long way up, at the top of Mount Kilimanjaro (kih-lih-mun-JAR-oh).

Kilimanjaro is the highest mountain in Africa. It is a dormant, or sleeping, volcano, which means it has not erupted in a very long time.

Lake Victoria

Lake Victoria is the largest lake in Africa. Part of it is in Tanzania. Two other African countries (Kenya and Uganda) also border Lake Victoria, which was named after a queen of England. Lake Victoria is near the Great Rift Valley.

The Great Rift Valley is a 6,000-mile long crack in the Earth's crust. It was formed about 20 million years ago by violent underground forces that tore the Earth's surface apart. The Great Rift Valley stretches across several African countries, including Tanzania and Kenya.

Animals and the Great Migration

Millions of African animals roam the plains of Tanzania. There are zebras and gazelles, flamingos and giraffes, rhinoceroses and hippopotamuses.

The plains are very dry during parts of the year. During these **droughts**, animals move to better feeding ground. More than a million animals **migrate** north, closer to Lake Victoria, where there is more food for them to eat. These animals travel about 500 miles.

Some animals are too weak or sick to make this long trip. Lions, cheetahs, and leopards **prey** on these animals. Vultures swoop down after a kill to finish cleaning the bones.

Ngorongoro Crater

The Ngorongoro (en-gor-un-GOH-roh) Crater is a unique natural feature. Scientists believe that a very

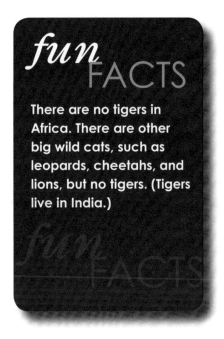

fun FACTS

There are no tigers in Africa. There are other big wild cats, such as leopards, cheetahs, and lions, but no tigers. (Tigers live in India.)

fun FACTS

Ngorongoro Crater is part of the Serengeti, whose name means "Endless Plains" in the Maasai language. Millions of animals, including wildebeest, zebras, antelope, and gazelles, migrate over the Serengeti twice a year.

long time ago, Ngorongoro volcano was as large as Mount Kilimanjaro. Then, after a big lava flow, the center of the volcano collapsed. After the crater cooled, millions of animals came there to live.

The land inside the crater was more **fertile** than other parts of Tanzania. There was more grass for the animals to eat. More grass eaters brought more **predators**.

Zebras inside the Ngorongoro Crater. Their shiny fur reflects sunlight and helps keep them cool on the hot African plains. The stripes break up the outline of their body and act like a kind of camouflage, making it harder for predators to catch them.

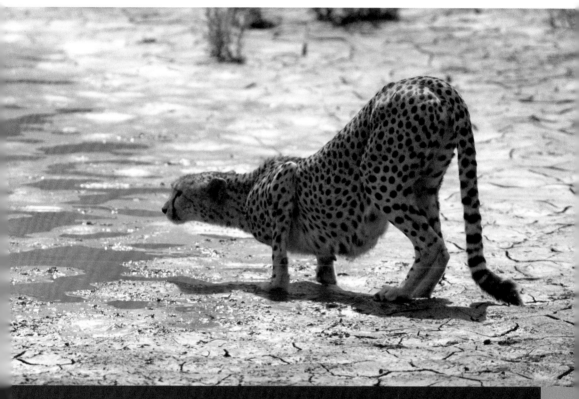

The cheetah is the fastest land animal. It is a big wild cat. Cheetahs range from about 90 pounds to as much as 140 pounds. Their bodies are about 4 feet long and their tails can grow to be more than two and a half feet long.

Maasai people also used to live in the crater. Now that area is reserved for tourist safaris.

Cheetahs hunt freely. They chase down their prey by running as fast as a speeding car. But they cannot run this fast for long, and they cannot change direction quickly. If the cheetah's prey makes several sharp turns, the cheetah will tire before it can make the kill.

Maasai women shave their heads, as do the men and children. Marriage is one of the most important events in a woman's life. It brings safety and security and, most importantly, children. The Maasai believe that to die without having children is a tragedy.

Village
Life

Chapter **4**

Tanzania is a poor country. Many Tanzanians do not have enough food to eat or clean water to drink. There are a few big cities in Tanzania, but more than half of all Tanzanians live in villages. There are hospitals in the cities, but there are no doctors in villages. Most people do not get to see a doctor regularly.

Tanzanian people belong to different groups. Each group has its own tribal language. Groups have different traditions and customs, too. Many of these groups, including the Maasai people, live in villages and raise cows.

Within the villages, people live together in family groups. Men can have more than one wife, but each wife will live in her own hut with her young children.

A Tanzanian village is called a **boma** (boh-mah), or sometimes *kraal* or *enkang*. (A hut is also called a *boma*.) The women build simple huts using wood and mud. The huts are built in a circle, facing in. They are small and dark inside. People do not spend a lot of time in their huts; they use them only for sleeping. A simple fence made with branches from thorn bushes surrounds the village. This keeps cows and goats in, and wild animals, like lions and leopards, out.

Villages do not have running water or flush toilets. Girls and women collect water every day. They fill plastic buckets or jugs with runoff from the mountains or another source. Then they carry the heavy jugs of water on their head all the way home. Much of Tanzania is dry. People do not waste water.

Maasai women build their own huts without any help from the men. They sleep inside with their young children on wooden beds covered with cowhides. A *boma* may last for five years or longer before it will need to be rebuilt.

Girls help their mothers with household chores. Getting water for cooking, washing, and drinking is a big job. The source for the water can be a long walk from the boma.

There is no electricity in villages. Cities may be wired for electricity, but it does not work all the time. Some people have radios that run on batteries, but there are no television sets. There are few cars. Some men use bicycles for transportation. If a place is too far away to walk, you can pay a little to hop on a *daladala*. This is usually an old minivan that works as a shared taxi.

Daladala are minivans that operate like local buses. *Daladala* do not run on a schedule. They will leave only when they are full, so there may be a wait of a few hours. People cram in, sitting on each others' laps when the seats are full.

People can buy fruits and vegetables at little stands. There are no big stores. Soap is a luxury. Instead of toothbrushes, people chew on a special kind of tree branch. As they chew on the branch, the wood becomes like the bristles on a toothbrush. People carry these sticks with them to chew. The wood has no taste, but it does help keep their teeth clean and healthy.

What Time Is It?

Most people in Tanzania do not own a clock or a watch. Time is not as important to them as it is to people in many other countries.

In Tanzania, the sun rises and sets at about the same time every day. In the United States, a person may get up at eight o'clock in the morning. Americans count the hours from midnight. But in Tanzania, people count the hours from sunrise, when they get up. What Americans would call noon is the sixth hour of their day in Tanzania, because the sun has been up for six hours.

School

School starts at about 8:00 A.M., which is two hours after sunrise. The children line up outside the school. They sing a school song and the national song, or a song from their region. All children wear uniforms to school. If the family does not have money to buy a uniform, the child cannot go to school. However, most children only own one uniform, which can get very

Maasai boys and girls go to school together. Different schools have different uniforms.

Saitoti, in the bottom photo, is not wearing his school uniform. He just stopped in to say goodbye to his classmates before leaving for the United States.

ripped and worn over the school year. A student can still attend school while a new uniform is being made.

Children speak their tribal language at home. They learn Swahili at school. The teacher writes on the board. Children copy what is on the board into a notebook. The teacher makes sure that they are copying correctly. They do not have schoolbooks. There is no homework, because there are no books to take home. There are also no report cards.

Students take a test to get into high school, where they can learn English. Very few pass the test. However, even those who do pass the test may not have the money to go.

The Maasai

The Maasai are **nomads**. They move from place to place to graze their cattle. **Herding** is a very important part of Maasai culture. The Maasai believe that all cattle originally belonged to their people, so if any other groups have cattle, they feel it must have been stolen from the Maasai. The Maasai used to raid other

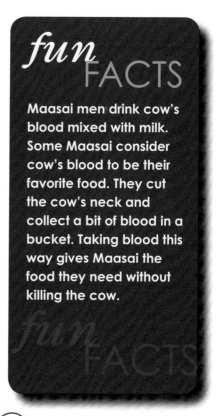

fun FACTS

Maasai men drink cow's blood mixed with milk. Some Maasai consider cow's blood to be their favorite food. They cut the cow's neck and collect a bit of blood in a bucket. Taking blood this way gives Maasai the food they need without killing the cow.

villages to "take back" their cattle. These cattle raids are now against the law.

Usually, only boys herd. However, if a family has no sons, a girl might herd. To teach them how to care for the animals, very young children are put in charge of a baby goat. As they get older, they are put in charge of more and more animals. By the time a boy is six or

The Maasai name their cows, and call each by name. Cows are used like money, but they are more than just valuable property. The Maasai are "people of cattle." Herding is considered a pleasant and noble way to spend time, even for Maasai warriors.

There are many cultures in Tanzania other than the Maasai. Muslims in Zanzibar celebrate several holidays with music and dancing. Besides religious holidays, they also celebrate Zanzibar Revolution Day (January 12) and Independence Day (December 9).

seven, he may be in charge of twenty cows. They take the animals outside the village to graze. They must move the cows to where there is food and water. Sometimes they must scare off a lion using only a herding stick or spear. It is a serious responsibility to return the cows or goats safely at the end of the day.

Jack hoped that Saitoti would want to play soccer. Would he know how to play?

Jambo Means "Hello"

Chapter 5

"*Jambo, Saitoti!*" the class said together as the new boy entered the class. The children had learned a few Swahili words as they studied Tanzania. *Jambo* (JAH-mbow) means "hello."

Saitoti smiled but did not say anything.

"He may not speak English," said Luke.

"I just hope he plays soccer," Jack said.

Ms. Griffith showed Saitoti where to sit. A teacher's aide named Jane sat next to him. She was going to help him learn English. The class had already learned a few Swahili words. They learned the names of African animals. Stacey showed Saitoti the poster they had made. He said each word in Swahili. Then he practiced saying the English words.

Lisa brought out some beaded necklaces the class had made as a welcome gift. They had learned that Maasai men and women wear this kind of jewelry. Saitoti had brought small gifts for his classmates. too. He gave each of them a small, carved elephant.

Saitoti shared these photos with his new American classmates. They show his family and his mother's boma. Saitoti's little sister cannot walk. He brought back a stroller from America so that his mother would not have to continue to carry her.

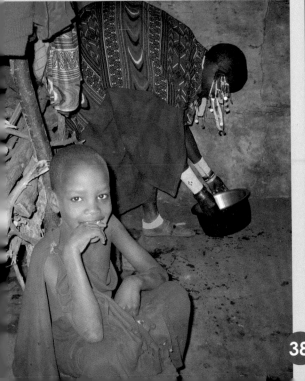

English	Swahili
cheetah	*duma* (DOO-mah)
elephant	*tembo* (TEM-boh)
hippopotamus	*kiboko* (ki-BOH-koh)
lion	*simba* (SIM-bah)
ostrich	*mbuni* (mm-BOO-nee)
zebra	*punda milia* (POON-dah mee-LEE-ah)

"Tembo," Stacey said.

"El-uh-funt," said Saitoti.

Ms. Griffith passed out small pieces of maple candy, which was made near the school. She wanted Saitoti to have a taste of Vermont. Jack remembered a class trip to the sugarhouse last March. They had seen how the sap from maple trees was boiled down to make syrup. Maple candy was also made from the sap, but it was even sweeter than the syrup.

As they finished their candy, Jack glanced at the clock. Only ten minutes till recess. He had brought a soccer ball with him to school that morning. He and Luke had a plan. They would invite Saitoti to play soccer with them.

When the bell rang, Jack jumped out of his seat. In a flash, he was standing in front of the new boy. "Would you like to play with us?" he asked, speaking slowly. Saitoti smiled and followed Jack out into the schoolyard. Luke was already kicking the ball around. He kicked it softly to Saitoti.

Saitoti told us about a traditional jumping dance that Maasai warriors perform. They jump straight up in the air from a standing position. It is like a contest to see who can jump the highest. Some men can jump as high as three or four feet off the ground.

Saitoti caught the ball skillfully with one foot, passed it to his other foot, and tapped it into the air.

"He plays soccer!" said Jack. He hoped their new student would want to join their team.

How To Make
Ugali

Ugali is a basic food for many Tanzanians. It is easy to make and quite filling. Ugali does not have much taste. In Tanzania, it is sometimes served with a sauce made with greens, or with meat or soured milk. Although the local people eat it often, it is not very popular with tourists who visit from other parts of the world.

People in Tanzania just eat ugali from the pan, using their hands. They eat it plain, or they use it to scoop other food, such as greens or meats. You can serve it on a plate or tray.

Things You Will Need

An adult
Pan
Stove
Spoon
Large plate or serving tray

Ingredients

2 cups fine white cornmeal

4 cups water (more or less, depending on how thick you want your ugali)

2 teaspoons salt

Instructions

1. **With the help of an adult**, boil the water and salt in a heavy saucepan.
2. Slowly add the cornmeal.
3. **Have the adult** lower the heat and stir out the lumps.
4. After cooking for about ten minutes, the porridge should thicken. **Have the adult** take the pan off the heat.
5. When it is cool, form the ugali into balls. Make sure your hands are wet (and clean) when you do this so that the ugali does not stick to your fingers.

Make Your Own
Tanzanian
Beaded Necklace

You Will Need

Beads

Beading thread

Beading Needle

Maasai men and women wear beaded necklaces. Some necklaces are wide with many strands of beads. Only the women do beadwork. They also make earrings and bracelets. Sometimes they sew the beads onto animal skins and clothing.

Instructions for Making a Tanzanian Beaded Necklace

1. You can make a necklace or bracelet using beads and beading thread. When you choose colors for your necklace, remember that each color has a special meaning for the Maasai.

2. **Red** is the color of the Maasai people. It is a symbol for cow's blood, which is the lifeblood of the Maasai people.

   Blue is the color of the sky, which gives water for cows and people to drink. It is also a symbol for their gods who live up in the blue sky.

   Green is the color of grass, which feeds the cows. It is a symbol for health. The Maasai hope to grow as tall and beautiful as some green plants.

   Orange and **yellow** are "welcome" colors that symbolize kindness and hospitality.

   White is the color of milk and is a symbol of purity and health.

   Black is the color of the people. It is also a symbol for the hard times everyone goes through in life.

3. You can make your necklace any way you like. Using the needle and thread, string the beads in a pattern. Placing several beads of the same color together will make bands of color. Think about what each color means to the Maasai, and have fun as you make your necklace.

Further Reading

Books

Craats, Rennay. *Maasai (Indigenous Peoples)*. New York, Weigl Publishers, 2005.

Di Piazza, Francesca. *Tanzania in Pictures*. Visual Geography. Breckenridge, Colorado: Twenty-First Century Books, 2007.

MacDonald, Joan Vos. *Tanzania (Africa)*. Bromall, Pennsylvania: Mason Crest Publishers, 2004.

Murphy, Patricia J. *Tanzania (Countries of the World)*. Mankato, Minnesota: Bridgestone Books, 2002.

Ling, Chin Oi. *Welcome to Tanzania (Welcome to My Country)*. Strongsville, Ohio: Gareth Stevens Publishing, 2005.

On the Internet

Official Tanzania Web Site
    http://www.tanzania.go.tz/
PBS: The Ngorongoro Crater
    http://www.pbs.org/edens/ngorongoro/index.html

Works Consulted

To write this book, the author relied on information from friends who taught school in Tanzania and are currently the guardians for a Tanzanian boy. The boy was the inspiration for the boy from Tanzania in this book.

Amin, Mohamed, et al. *The Last of the Maasai*. Nairobi: Camperapix Publishers International, 1987.

Gilbert, Elizabeth L. *Broken Spears: A Maasai Journey*. New York: Atlantic Monthly Press, 2003.

Lekuton, Joseph Lemasolai, and Herman Viola. *Facing the Lion: Growing Up Maasai on the African Savanna*. Washington, D.C.: National Geographic Children's Books, 2005.

Mercer, Graham. "Tanzania Takes the Breath Away." *New African*, June 2007.

Ndaskoi, Navaya ole. "Tanzania: The Maasai Predicament." *New African*, June 2003.

Phillips, Jaqueline S. "Maasai's Education and Empowerment: Challenges of a Migrant Lifestyle." *Childhood Education*, Spring 2002.

Further Reading

Saitoti, Tepihit Ole. *The Worlds of the Maasai Warrior* (Autobiography). Berkeley: University of California Press, 1988.
Saitoti, Tepihit Ole, and Carol Beckwith. *Maasai*. New York: Abradale Press (Harry N. Abrams, Inc. Publishing), 1990.
Spear, Thomas, and Richard Waller (editors). *Being Maasai: Ethnicity & Identity in East Africa*. London: James Currey, 1993.

Embassy

Embassy of The United Republic of Tanzania
2139 R Street, NW
Washington, DC 20008
Telephone: (202) 939-6125
             (202) 884-1080
Fax: (202) 797-7408
http://www.tanzaniaembassy-us.org/

Tanzanian shilling notes

Glossary

boma (BOH-muh)—A Maasai hut or village.

capitalism (KAA-pih-tul-ism)—An economic system based on big business.

daladala (daa-lah-daa-lah)—A shared taxi.

domestic (doh-MES-tik)—Tame, for keeping at home either as a pet or livestock.

drought (DROWT)—A long time with little or no rain.

economy (ee-KAH-nuh-mee)—The flow of goods and money.

equator (ee-KWAY-tur)—An imaginary line around the middle of the earth, halfway between the North and South Poles.

fertile (FER-tul)—Able to produce healthy plants.

fossils (FAA-suls)—Animal or plant remains that have been preserved in rock.

herding (HER-ding)—Keeping a group of animals together.

independent (in-dee-PEN-dent)—Having the power to self-govern.

Islam (IZ-lahm)—The religion of the Muslims that teaches there is one God, Allah, and that Muhammad is his prophet.

migrate (MY-grayt)—To move from one place to another, following jobs, food, or the seasons.

Muslim (MUZ-lim)—A person who practices the religion of Islam.

national (NAA-shuh-nul)—Of a country.

nomads (NOH-madz)—People who wander from place to place, following good weather or hunting grounds; they do not have permanent homes.

plains (PLAINS)—Flat land on which grasses grow.

political party (poh-LIH-tih-kul PAR-tee)—A group of people who work together to promote one type of government.

ports (PORTS)—Places where ships can rest safely at anchor.

predators (PREH-duh-turs)—Animals that hunt other animals for food.

prey (PRAY)—Animals captured by other animals for food.

safari (suh-FAR-ee)—A journey to find animals in the wild, especially in Africa.

socialist (SOH-shul-ist))—An economic system in which the government owns everything; there is no private ownership.

sultans (SUL-tuns)—Muslim rulers who were like kings.

Swahili (swah-HEE-lee)—A language spoken by millions of people in Africa.

tribal (TRY-bul)—Belonging to a tribe, or group, of people.

Index

ABOUT THE AUTHOR

Ann Weil has written more than 50 books for children. The idea for this book came from the author's experience when a Maasai boy from Tanzania joined her daughter's first-grade class. Leyeyo spoke very little English when he arrived, but he could play soccer! As the children became friends, Ann had the opportunity to get to know his American guardians, Sarah Messenger (in photo below, left) and Paul Weber, who were teachers in Leyeyo's village of Longido in Tanzania. They and Leyeyo visit Longido each summer.

Leyeyo and author Ann Weil in Putney, Vermont

Sarah Messenger and a Maasai friend in Longido, Tanzania